NORTH-WEST ENGLAND FROM ABOVE

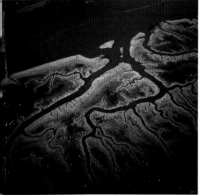

CONTENTS

GW00643315

INTRODUCTION

The north-west of England, for the purposes of this book, takes in five counties: Cumbria, Lancashire, Merseyside, Greater Manchester and Cheshire. Here we find the Lake District, one of the most picturesque areas in England, as well as key industrial areas such as Merseyside and Greater Manchester, and of course the famous holiday resort of Blackpool. The north-west's fine historical legacy includes stone circles, Hadrian's Wall and other Roman remains, castles and pele towers, priories, abbeys, cathedrals and fine Tudor houses.

The Lake District National Park covers 2,243 square km (866 square miles) and includes the principal English lakes and the highest English peaks. The valleys and lakes radiate from a central core of mountains containing some of the world's oldest rock formations. The geological structure is domelike, eroded by glacial action that deepened and widened existing valleys, while creating hanging valleys with attractive waterfalls. For a long time, this area was cut off from the outside world by its moorland, peat bogs and forest. The area only became accessible to significant numbers of tourists in the second half of the twentieth century when the road network was extended.

Today industry is concentrated in the south. In the early days of the Industrial Revolution, communities grew rapidly as the Mersey became a hub of activity. For centuries coal had been mined in Lancashire, and salt in Cheshire. Now the cotton industry developed from the wool trade. The world's first great railway opened in 1830, running from Manchester to Liverpool. This was supplemented by a network of canals to facilitate the movement of goods from the ports and between industrial centres. The Manchester Ship Canal opened in 1894 making Manchester an inland port.

Photographs from top to bottom: Hadrian's Wall, Castlerigg Stone Circle, mud flats on the River Lune, Liverpool

Photographs, text and design by Adrian Warren and Dae Sasitorn

MYRIAD BOOKS LIMITED

The region is rich in history. Four thousand years ago Bronze Age settlers in Cumbria and Westmorland built the magnificent stone circle at Castlerigg. The Romans controlled the region for four hundred years until the fifth century. Early in the 7th century, the Anglian empire expanded into Northumbria. The Celtic people of Cumbria and Wales (known as the Cymry, or compatriots) were divided following a battle at Chester in 615, which left most of Cumbria under Anglian control. We can still see Anglian elements such as -tun, meaning a farmstead, in Cumbrian placenames (for example Clifton and Brampton).

The ninth century saw second and third generation Vikings come from Ireland and the Isle of Man to settle in Cumbria. Their presence in the area is still felt in place-names, local folklore and the dialect of the Cumbrian people, as well as carved stone crosses in several churches and churchyards. By the early tenth century, much of Cumbria was under the control of the English King Edmund I. He gave Cumbria to Malcolm I of Scotland in return for his support in defending northern Britain against the Vikings. For the next eight centuries the ownership of Carlisle and what we know today as Cumbria would continually change between the Scots and the English. This was finally resolved in 1745 when the English drove out Bonnie Prince Charlie's troops.

****

HADRIAN'S WALL
Housesteads Roman Fort, and the wall to the west (left)

Between AD121 and 125, Emperor Hadrian toured the frontiers of his empire. In order to put an end to attacks from the north and to guard Rome's north-west frontier, he decided to build a wall 117km (73 miles) long, as a fortification. It crossed the neck of England, from the mouth of the River Tyne in the east to the Solway Firth in the west. Bowness on Solway (Maia) marks the end of the wall in the west but few remains are visible. It followed the crest of ridges, and steep sides facing north added to the impregnability of the barrier. Construction took over seven years, requiring vast resources and manpower. The finished wall was guarded by up to 12,000 men: there were sixteen forts along its length and, between these, mile castles and turrets. Housesteads fort is close to the halfway point along the wall, just inside today's Northumberland, and has the most impressive remains of all the forts. Hadrian's Wall is without doubt the most important monument left by the Romans in Britain, invoking a dramatic image of a country divided by conflict and occupation. It has been declared a World Heritage Site.

****

CARLISLE
Cumbria (above)

Today, Carlisle (from Carleol, the old Celtic name) is the capital of the county of Cumbria, but its position close to the border of Scotland has made the city strategically important throughout British history. In AD78 the Roman governor Agricola built Luguvalium, a wood and turf fort on the site where the castle now stands. The fort later became the Roman town of Luguvadio, which now lies buried beneath the modern city centre.

Carlisle Castle overlooks the River Eden. Once a prison for Mary Queen of Scots, it was built in 1092. Despite falling temporarily into Scottish possession during the Civil War, and later during the Jacobite Rising, Carlisle has remained an English possession since the 12th century. Carlisle Cathedral is the second smallest in England. Originally a Norman priory church, it became a cathedral in 1133. Today, it houses medieval carvings and one of the finest examples of 14th century stained-glass windows in the country.

****

WETHERAL, Cumbria (above)

Wetheral, just 8km (5 miles) east of Carlisle, is a picturesque village, with pleasant walks by the River Eden in National Trust woodland. A Benedictine priory was founded here in the 15th century but only the gatehouse remains. The Gothic church of the Holy Trinity is said to be 15th century. The viaduct was built between 1830-34 for the old North Eastern Railway.

****

<u>THE RIVER EDEN FLOWING INTO THE SOLWAY FIRTH</u>, Cumbria (above)

The river rises on the Cumbria-Yorkshire border and flows northwards to Carlisle before emptying into the Solway Firth. The eastern part of the catchment is drained by short, steep streams from the Pennines, while the western part includes tributaries which flow from the Lake District. The river is excellent for salmon fishing and also supports sea trout, crayfish and otters.

****

<u>STONE WALLS NEAR WASDALE HEAD</u>, Cumbria (above)

Dry-stone walls are, together with hedgerows, one of the most commonly used field boundaries in England. They help create the traditional pattern of fields and lanes so evocative of our rural landscape. As landowners abandoned farming in favour of raising sheep and cattle, they needed to control their livestock. So they enclosed land which had been previously used as common land by all the local inhabitants. Although most of the dry-stone walls that form the boundaries of fields date from around 200 years ago, some have origins stretching from the 12th century, and the technique of dry-stone walling can be traced as far back as the Iron Age.

****

SCAFELL PIKE, Cumbria (left)

At 978m Scafell Pike is the highest peak in England and is very closely connected to nearby Scafell, just 13m lower. It is considered one of the most difficult of climbs in the Lake District with a more jagged promontory than Skiddaw mountain. The gentlest ascents are from the Borrowdale side or from Wasdale Head. The climb is very rewarding, with stunning views over Wastwater to the west and the Langdale Pikes to the east. A friend of the poet Wordsworth, Southey, made the first recorded climb in 1802.

****

MOUNTAIN RIDGES, LAKE DISTRICT
Cumbria (below)

The view from Derwent Fells, looking north-west towards a succession of valleys and mountain ridges, includes Brackenthwaite Fell (851m) and Grisedale Pike (790m).

****

CASTLERIGG – STONE CIRCLE
Cumbria (left)

Some five thousand years ago Castlerigg stone circle was built of 38 unworked boulders of variable sizes and shapes, some standing over 1.5m in height. This is not however a true circle, since the north-eastern side is flattened. Just inside the eastern end of the circle is a group of 10 stones that form a rectangular enclosure or cove. Excavations in the cove in 1882 revealed quantities of charcoal and, in 1875, a stone axehead was found at the site. Many of the stones of Castlerigg seem to reflect features in the surrounding hills, suggesting a link between the sacred space and the landscape beyond.

****

KESWICK AND DERWENTWATER
Cumbria (above, and top left next page)

Keswick, with its narrow streets and buildings of grey stone, has a beautiful setting on Derwentwater, below the mountains of Skiddaw and Saddleback. It is the northern centre for the Lakes and attracts visitors from all over the world. The original settlement was at Crosthwaite, on the western side of the town, where St Kentigern's church was built in the 6th century. During the reign of Elizabeth I, the rural economy was transformed when minerals, including copper were discovered in Newlands and Borrowdale. Later in the 16th century black lead was discovered at Seathwaite, and the resulting pencilmaking industry is still a mainstay of the town.

****

<u>KESWICK</u>, Cumbria
(above – see caption previous page)

<u>LAKE CONISTON</u>
Cumbria (right)

Coniston Water is overlooked by the mountain Coniston Old Man (803m) a favourite with hill walkers, and Dow Crag, with its 183m wall offering some of the best rock climbing in Britain. The Victorian steam yacht Gondola ferries passengers around the lake along with two traditional 1920s timber launches. Coniston Water witnessed the death of Donald Campbell in 1967 in his attempt to break the world water speed record in the legendary Bluebird. The village of Coniston lies at the northern end. Norsemen settled here over a thousand years ago, but in the 18th and the 19th centuries Coniston suddenly grew with the wealth from local coppermines and some of the largest slate quarries in the Lake District.

****

LAKE DISTRICT VALLEY NORTH OF THIRLMERE
Cumbria (above)

A typical verdant valley in the Lake District, with its patchwork of fields bounded on either side by steep wild moorland.

****

STAINTON FELL
Cumbria (right)

The view from Stainton Fell looking west towards Ravenglass, the mouth of the River Esk and the Irish Sea.

****

<u>LAKE WINDERMERE</u>, Cumbria

At 17km (over 10 miles) in length, Windermere is England's largest lake. It is not really a mountain lake: its southern end is set in mild countryside and it's only the northern end, at **Ambleside** (left), that is among mountain scenery. **Bowness and the town of Windermere** (above) are situated on the eastern shore of the lake and are now, like Ambleside, popular resorts. In Roman times, Ambleside was on the road from Ravenglass and Hardknott to Penrith, and the fort of Galava stood between the site of the present town and the lake. Roman remains have also been found on Belle Isle opposite Bowness. Like Ambleside, Bowness became a settlement with the arrival of the Vikings. They knew the lake as

Vinander's Mere, a name which over the centuries became Windermere.

The lake has been a water highway for centuries for the transport of goods to lakeside communities but the arrival of the railway in 1847 brought prosperity: new trades and employment opportunities came to the inhabitants; grand hotels and large houses were built for wealthy people who could now commute to places such as Barrow, Carlisle, and Lancaster. Local industrialists who made fortunes during the Industrial Revolution chose to live in the area, and many of their former homes are now sumptuous hotels.

****

KENDAL and ITS CASTLE
Cumbria (above)

Kendal has a rich history. The ruined Norman castle at Castle Hill was the birthplace of Catherine Parr, Henry VIII's sixth wife and the only one to survive him. Her prayer book, bound in silver, is kept in the town hall. In 1331 Flemish workers settled in Kendal and established a wool-weaving industry. Today, modern and traditional industries work alongside each other making a wide range of products from snuff to shoes, as well as the world famous Kendal Mint Cake. Kendal's historic Friends Meeting House is home to the Quaker Tapestry. More than 4,000 people from 15 different countries collaborated to produce this stunning tapestry, which illustrates nearly 350 years of social history.

****

PELE TOWERS, Cumbria

Edward I fought a long and bitter campaign to conquer Scotland. The Scots resisted with armies of up to 40,000 men, destroying farms and churches, plundering abbeys, slaughtering people and cattle in the Lake District. Determined to resist further invasion, the people of Cumberland and Westmorland built defensive structures known as pele towers, unique to the north of England. These were small stone buildings with walls from one to three metres thick, square or oblong in shape. Designed to withstand short sieges, they usually consisted of three storeys. The tunnel-vaulted ground floor had no windows and was used as a storage area and to accommodate animals. The first floor contained a hall and kitchen, and the top floor was space for living and sleeping. The roof with its battlements was normally flat for lookout purposes, to allow arrows to be fired and missiles to be hurled down on raiders.

DACRE (above) built in the 13th century, is one of the most perfect pele towers. In the 7th century there was a monastery in the village, and the church has 9th-century cross-shafts. Earthworks at Dacre Castle are thought to be where Constantine of Scotland and Eugenius of Cumberland signed a treaty with Athelstan of England in 927.

Ivo, grandson of local Saxon chieftain Llyulph, created the first stone structure on the site of **GREYSTOKE CASTLE** (left) in 1129. This building grew to become one of the border chain of fortifications. In 1338 William de Greystoke obtained a royal licence to castellate the huge pele tower. The castle's 2428 ha (6000 acres) are said to be the largest enclosure in England with no road or right of way running through it.

****

PIEL CASTLE, Cumbria (previous page)

Piel Island was first visited by Celts and Romans and later settled by Scandinavians. This fortress was built in the 14th century to stand guard over Barrow harbour, which was once considered the best between Milford Haven in Wales and the Scottish border. King John first allowed Furness Abbey to store provisions on the island in 1212. Thereafter, ships under royal protection used the island to unload cargo destined for the abbey and this resulted in a roaring smuggling trade. Today, only the overgrown remains of the castle, an inn and a few primitive 18th-century homes without electricity dot the island. The landlord of the lonely Ship Inn is the only permanent resident; he is traditionally known as the King of Piel.

****

BARROW IN FURNESS, Cumbria (below)

On the southern tip of the Furness and Cartmel peninsula lies Barrow-in-Furness, the largest town in the south of Cumbria. Its name comes from the Celtic "barr" and the Old Scandinavian "ey", meaning "promontory island". The name Furness means "rump-shaped headland" from the Old Scandinavian words "futh" and "nes". Barrow evolved because it offered a safe harbour sheltered by Walney Island, and it was close to the rich deposits of iron ore in the Furness mines. It was a small village until the railway arrived in 1846, bringing prosperity and growth. Soon, the town was one of England's leading ports with a major shipbuilding industry and the largest ironworks in the world. Today Barrow is a busy town with a population of more than 60,000.

****

WIND FARM AT KIRKBY MOOR
Cumbria (left)

The Kirkby Moor wind farm first started operating in 1993, and generates enough clean electricity every year to meet the needs of about 4,000 homes. Conventional methods of generating that much electricity would produce around 10,000 tonnes of carbon dioxide annually. Energy generated by wind farms does not release carbon dioxide, a main contributor to global warming and climate change.

****

<u>SELLAFIELD</u>, Cumbria (below)

Sellafield, formerly Windscale, occupies just 3 square kms on the Irish Sea coast alongside the Lake District. The controversial site houses two types of nuclear installation: one providing electricity for the national grid, and the other reprocessing spent nuclear fuel. Ironically, in spite of public concern over the site's safety, Sellafield remains one of the north west's most popular tourist destinations.

****

<u>BLACKPOOL</u>, Lancashire (above)

Blackpool is famous as a holiday resort and the 158m tower is its most prominent landmark. The shoreline bristles with piers, a giant rollercoaster ride, amusement arcades, tram and donkey rides, pubs, fish and chip shops, casinos, bingo halls and nightclubs. The resort is also known for its illuminations: from the beginning of September to November, over half a million light bulbs decorate the promenade.

****

<u>MORECAMBE BAY</u>, Lancashire (right)

Morecambe Bay has Britain's largest continuous area of intertidal mud flats and sand flats. In size, the bay is second only to the Wash. The marine habitats are diverse, from fringing salt marsh and sand and tidal mud flats, to dense beds of mussels which can cover the surface of every available boulder and cobble. It is also important for birds, with pink-footed geese, shelduck, pintail, oystercatcher, grey plover, knot, dunlin and many others.

****

LANCASTER CASTLE
Lancashire (left)

LANCASTER FROM THE MUD FLATS OF THE RIVER LUNE,
Lancashire (below)

Parts of a Roman church dating from the second century were discovered at Lancaster in 1912. Roman lamps bearing the markings XP (the first two letters of Christos, Christ in Greek) were unearthed in the vicarage garden. The 11th century castle was built with materials taken from a late Roman fort. At the beginning of the English Civil War, Lancaster Castle was surrendered to the Parliamentarians without a shot being fired. There have been many famous trials and executions at the castle: more death sentences were handed down here than at any other court in England except for Old Newgate in London. Crowds of several thousand people used to turn up to watch public executions outside the castle. The last execution in Lancaster, which was not in public, was in 1910.

****

BURNLEY
Lancashire (left)

Burnley has done much in the past decades to shed its mill town image. New industries now take the place of the old. The town was once known as the greatest cotton-manufacturing place in Britain and at one time boasted over 100,000 looms.

****

PRESTON
Lancashire (below)

In the 18th century, Preston was at the heart of the Industrial Revolution. The introduction of machinery, bad harvests and the Corn Laws brought riots to Lancashire and destruction of machinery by those who saw their livelihoods threatened by the introduction of machines. Richard Arkwright, born in Preston in 1732, invented the spinning frame in 1769 to cheapen cotton production but had to move to Nottingham to avoid attacks. John Horrocks set up the first cotton mill in Preston and the town became an important centre for the industry.

****

BOLTON
Greater Manchester (left)

The history of this busy industrial town goes back to before the Norman conquest, but it was the cotton industry that brought the town to prominence. Bolton grew into one of the largest boroughs in Lancashire but today many of the old mills house other industries. During the Civil War, the town witnessed a bloody massacre by Royalists, as a result of which the Earl of Derby, James Stanley, was beheaded by Cromwell.

****

WIGAN
Greater Manchester (below)

Coal has been mined in the Wigan area for centuries. While some Roman workings have been found, coal mining is first mentioned in a document dated 1330. Since then more than 700 million tons of coal have been extracted. There are probably well over 1,000 mineshafts in the Wigan area and 26 workable coal seams still exist. The last mine here closed in 1992 as a result of the national policy of closures and cheap imports. In the 19th century, Wigan was known as Coalopolis – the capital for coal.

****

MANCHESTER (above)

Since Roman times this area has been strategically important. Water power and good supplies of coal helped the development of the textile industries. In the early part of the 19th century commerce and industry grew rapidly but there was appalling squalor, moral degradation and poverty among people living in congested areas of the city. The Manchester ship canal opened in 1894, making the city an inland port. Today Greater Manchester is one of the most densely populated areas in England and second only to London in its importance as a commercial, financial and banking centre.

****

EDGE OF THE PEAK DISTRICT (left)

The edge of the Peak District near Whaley Bridge is very close to the eastern edge of Greater Manchester. The Peak District National Park is an area of outstanding natural beauty and in 1951 this was the first to be designated a national park. The southern part consists of rolling limestone uplands and wooded dales while to the north is moorland.

****

ROCHDALE
Greater Manchester (above)

This old mill town is situated high up near the Pennine moors. Its original source of industrial prosperity until the end of the 18th century was wool. However cotton took over when many cotton mills were built during the 19th century. After the industry suffered a series of slumps, some local men combined forces to establish the first ever co-operative society in 1844. Today the industries at Rochdale are varied and the skyline is dominated by square tower blocks of flats. Judging from the many flints and Bronze Age implements discovered, the Rochdale area has long been a centre of population. There is a remarkably well preserved section of a Roman road up on the moors at Blackstone Edge.

****

BURY, Greater Manchester (right)

The manufacture of cotton, bleaching and calico printing in the early 19th brought prosperity to Bury and the surrounding area. John Kay, inventor of the flying shuttle, was born in Bury. Bury's most famous son is Robert Peel. Born in 1788, he was the founder of the modern police force and later became prime minister. In 1841, he repealed the Corn Laws. He was also the first to impose income tax in time of peace.

****

LIVERPOOL, Merseyside (above)

The waterfront of Liverpool is dominated by big buildings: the Liver, Cunard and the Harbour Board. This was once Europe's greatest Atlantic seaport with miles of docks and the world's largest floating landing stage. Liverpool began as a fishing village in the 13th century but grew rapidly during the 18th century as a result of the Industrial Revolution. As well as industry, it is renowned for its flourishing musical and artistic traditions. The city has two modern cathedrals: the Catholic cathedral of Christ the King was consecrated in 1967; the red sandstone Anglican cathedral, finished in 1978, is second in size only to St. Peter's in Rome.

****

BIRKENHEAD, Merseyside (right)

A priory was founded here in the 12th century when land was granted to the Benedictine Black Monks. This secluded spot near the head of the Wirral peninsula was screened by forests. Until the 19th century, Birkenhead was a quiet hamlet, relatively untroubled by the post-Dissolution upheavals. From 1817 a steam ferry opened the area up to settlers from the northern side of the Mersey. The first docks opened in 1847 and these, combined with shipbuilding, significantly influenced the development of the area. The Mersey rail tunnel opened in 1886 and the road tunnel in 1934.

****

CREWE
Cheshire (above)

Crewe is perhaps best known as a major hub for the British railway system. In 1837 the village became the junction of three railway lines: the Manchester & Birmingham, the Great Junction and the Chester & Crewe. Other railway companies also built lines to Crewe: the North Staffordshire (1848), Great Western (1863) and the Midland (1867). In 1840 the Great Junction company purchased the Chester & Crewe Railway and large areas of land in Crewe. The company then moved its locomotive and carriage works from Liverpool to the town. For the next 150 years, on average, one locomotive a week was manufactured here.

****

<u>BEESTON CASTLE</u>, Cheshire (left)

The medieval ruins of Beeston Castle stand on a rocky summit 150m above the Cheshire plain. There are wonderful views on all sides, from the Pennines in the east to the mountains of Wales in the west. The fortification dates from 1225 when it was built by Ranulf, the sixth Earl of Chester, with one of the deepest castle wells in the country. The castle was seized by Henry III in 1237 and he and his son, Edward I, used it as a base for their campaigns against the Welsh. The castle was finally destroyed at the end of the Civil War. Archaeological excavations have revealed the remains of a Bronze Age community living on the Beeston crag about 800BC, and other excavations have discovered a later Iron Age hill fort. The hill fort was probably abandoned at the beginning of the Roman period.

****

<u>CHESTER</u>, Cheshire (above)

In AD70, Chester was the fortress of the 20th Roman legion, Valeria Victrix, charged with suppressing the army of the warrior queen, Boadicea. The massive harbour and border position made it an important strategic outpost. After the Romans withdrew however, the city fell prey to marauding Danes and Saxons and was virtually derelict by 900. The Normans reached Chester in about 1070. They built Chester Castle and, by the Middle Ages, it was once more an affluent and prosperous port. During the 15th century, however, the River Dee began to silt up and the seaborne trade faded. Over the centuries, the Roman walls have remained virtually intact. The city still boasts distinctive medieval features, in particular double-level walkways with a continuous line of balconies known as The Rows.

****

LITTLE MORETON HALL
Cheshire (left)

Here is a unique national treasure. The striking black and white timber-framed building of Little Moreton Hall stands beside the clear, still waters of its moat. The original house was built over 120 years by three generations of the Moreton family, starting in the mid-15th century. They owned it for 500 years before presenting it to the National Trust in 1938. Look at Little Moreton Hall from any angle: you will find it difficult to see any part that is straight or square. Many of the glass panes appear blown and distorted under the weight of the heavy stone slate roof.

****

HOLMES CHAPEL
Cheshire (right)

The station at Holmes Chapel on the railway line from Crewe to Manchester is a small modern building to the east of the village. The line separates the village, which has been steadily growing since the opening of the railway in 1842. On the northern boundary of Holmes Chapel is the River Dane, which the railway crosses by a great viaduct built in 1840. The line is carried some 30m above the river, over twenty-three brick spans each 20m wide.

****

JODRELL BANK
Cheshire (right)

The story of Jodrell Bank began in 1945 when Bernard Lovell came to the University of Manchester to study cosmic rays. A quiet observation site away from city noise was required and the University's botanical station at Jodrell Bank, south of Manchester, was the ideal location. In 1947 a giant parabolic reflecting aerial was built. At over 66m, this was by far the largest radio telescope in the world at that time. The telescope enabled many important discoveries, notably radio noise from the Great Nebula in Andromeda – the first time that a known extra galactic radio source had been detected – and the remains of Tycho's supernova of 1572, which had no obvious visual remnant. These early successes established Jodrell Bank as a leading radio astronomy facility, and led to the building of an even larger and more versatile telescope.

****

WASTWATER, Cumbria (FRONT COVER)

In the Wasdale valley on the western fringe of the Lake District is the awe-inspiring Wastwater, at 79m the deepest lake in England. The steep scree slopes from Illgill Head plunge 518m to the lake bottom which lies below sea level. The lake is nearly 5km (3 miles) long, and almost 1km (half a mile) wide. Mountains surround the lake, Red Pike, Kirk Fell and Great Gable and Scafell Pike, England's highest. Norse farmers colonised the valley in the 9th and 10th centuries. At Wasdale Head is St. Olaf's church, one of the smallest in the country.

****

SOLWAY FIRTH, Cumbria (BACK COVER)

Opening out into the Irish Sea, the Solway Firth, 60 km (40 miles) long, marks the border between England and Scotland. It is fed from the north by numerous rivers including the Nith, Lochar, and Annan in Scotland, and, in England, the Rivers Esk, Eden and Waver. It is one of the least industrialised estuaries in Europe and an important area for birds, with salt marshes as well as the third largest area of continuous littoral mud flats and sand flats in the UK. The ruins of Hadrian's Wall can be traced as far west as Bowness on the south shore.

****

LAST REFUGE Ltd

Nature is a precious inheritance, to be cared for and cherished by all of us. Last Refuge Ltd is a small company primarily dedicated to documenting and archiving endangered environments and species in our rapidly changing world, through films, images and research. The company was established in 1992, while studying wild giant pandas in the Qinling mountains of central China, which seemed, literally, to be the "last refuge" for these charismatic animals. The company's name was adopted for that project and it seemed logical to continue with it, embracing new projects worldwide. Two films on lemurs in Madagascar quickly followed and the ring-tailed lemur became the company's logo. Adrian Warren and Dae Sasitorn, who run the company out of a farmhouse in Somerset, have created a special web site, www.lastrefuge.co.uk, in order to present their work, which is becoming a huge resource for information, and an extensive photographic archive of still and moving images for both education and media. Ultimately they hope to offer special conservation awards to fund work by others.

ADRIAN WARREN

Adrian Warren is a biologist, and a commercial pilot, with over thirty years experience as a photographer and filmmaker, working worldwide for the BBC Natural History Unit, and as a director in the IMAX giant screen format. He has recently designed a new wing mount camera system for aircraft to further develop his interest in aviation, aerial filming and photography. As a stills photographer, he has a personal photographic archive of over 100,000 pictures, with worldwide coverage of wildlife, landscapes, aerials, and peoples. His photographs appear in books, magazines, advertisements, posters, calendars, greetings cards and many other products. His awards include a Winston Churchill Fellowship; the Cherry Kearton Medal from the Royal Geographical Society in London; the Genesis award from the Ark Trust for Conservation;an International Prime Time Emmy; and the Golden Eagle Award from New York.

DAE SASITORN

Dae Sasitorn is an academic from the world of chemistry but has given it up to follow her love for nature. She manages the company and has created and designed the Last Refuge website as well as scanning thousands of images for the archive. She has also become a first-class photographer in her own right.

THE PHOTOGRAPHY

Adrian and Dae operate their own Cessna 182G out of a tiny farm strip close to their house. They bought the single engined four-seater aircraft in May 1999 in order to develop a new wing mounted camera system for cinematography. The 1964 Cessna was in beautiful condition, and had only one previous owner. It is the perfect aircraft for aerial work: small, manoeuvrable, with plenty of power, and the high wing configuration offering an almost unrestricted view on the world below. With twenty degrees of flap it is possible to fly as slowly as sixty knots. The cabin side window opens upwards and outwards and is kept open by the air flow. Over London, however, where it is not permitted to fly a single engine fixed wing aircraft in case of engine failure, the Cessna had to be abandoned in favour of a helicopter equipped with floats.

The photographs were taken on Hasselblad medium format 6x6cm cameras and lenses (mostly 50mm) using Fujichrome Velvia film. Waiting for the right weather, with a clear atmosphere and less than fifty per cent cloud cover, required being on standby for months.

First Published in 2009 by Myriad Books Limited,
35 Bishopsthorpe Road, London, SE26

Photographs and Text Copyright
Dae Sasitorn and Adrian Warren
Last Refuge Limited

Dae Sasitorn and Adrian Warren have asserted their right under the
Copyright, Designs and Patents Act, 1998, to be
identified as the authors of this work.

All rights reserved. No part of this publication may
be reproduced, stored on a retrieval system or
transmitted in any form or by any means, electronic,
mechanical, photocopying, recording or otherwise,
without the prior permission of the copyright owners.

ISBN 1 84746 230 8
EAN 978 1 84746 230 5

Designed by Dae Sasitorn and Adrian Warren
Last Refuge Limited
Printed in China